Your Life Without Debt

The Peace in Being Debt Free

By Frederick Weber

Copyright 2015 © All Rights Reserved

Except as permitted as under the U.S. Copyright Act of 1976, no part of this book may be copied, stored, reproduced, republished, uploaded, posted, transmitted, altered or distributed in any way, in whole or part in any form or any medium, or incorporated into any other work, without the express prior written permission except in the case of brief quotations embodied in critical reviews or articles.

Your support of the author's rights is appreciated.

The scanning, uploading and distribution of this book via the Internet or via any other means without the permission of the publisher is illegal and punishable by law. Please purchase only authorized electronic editions, and do not participate in or encourage electronic piracy of copyrighted materials.

Disclaimers:

The information provided within this book is for general informational purposes only. While we try to keep the information up-to-date and correct, there are no representations or warranties, express or implied, about the completeness, accuracy, reliability, suitability or availability with respect to the information, products, services, or related graphics contained in this book for any purpose. Any use of this information is at your own risk.

The author and publisher have made every effort to ensure the accuracy of the information within this book was correct at time of publication. The author and publisher do not assume and hereby disclaim any liability to any party for any loss, damage, or disruption caused by errors or omissions, whether such errors or omissions result from accident, negligence, or any other cause.

Table of Contents

Chapter 1: The World of Debt 1

Chapter 2: How Debt Impacts You 5

Chapter 3: Solving Your Debt Problem Without Borrowing.9

Chapter 4 – Debt Elimination Strategies 14

Chapter 5 – Benefits of working hard to become debt free19

Chapter 6 – Strategies for staying debt free 21

Conclusion 23

Chapter 1: The World of Debt

Debt seems to be a huge part of life. There are few people out there that are truly debt free - and far too many people find themselves shackled to debt for their entire lives. Understanding not only what debt is but how it is generated is an important lesson that is rarely imparted to children before it is too late. Falling into debt can be a passive or active action, but it's a dangerous trap into which anyone can fall given the right circumstances and the wrong training.

Why People Get in Debt Trouble

Debt can seem like something that happens to other people, especially if you're sitting in a place that's debt free. There are several reasons why it occurs, and many of those reasons start with very good intentions. We live in a society that's geared towards debt - it isn't just an unpleasant fact of life, but rather something that society actively encourages. From mortgage payments to student loans, it is expected that most people will have some kind of debt in their lives. What separates these so-called "good debts" from the usual "bad debts" is just the point of view of the people who collect on them. There are dozens of ways to go into debt, and some of them really aren't the fault of the people who find themselves there. Understanding how you get into debt is the first step towards getting yourself out of the world of debt and debt collectors.

It should come as no surprise that many people enter into debt because they are forced into situations where their needs outstrip their means. One of the most common sources of debt, as well as one of the most common causes of bankruptcy in the United States, is medical debt. If one does not have incredible health insurance, it's very easy to go in for a life-saving procedure and find that the bill will total in the tens of thousands of dollars. In these cases, it's impossible for the party going into debt to avoid those procedures - given a choice between death and debt, debt is always the preferable option. There are many other circumstances in which debt may be nearly unavoidable - losing a law suit, for example, can cause an individual to go into debt, as can sudden damage to a home after a natural disaster or even a car accident. When a person is unable to anticipate a major problem and is financially unprepared, the possibility of going into debt moves from the realm of the possible into something that is all too likely to actually occur.

Other people find themselves in debt because they simply don't understand how money works. It's sad but true that most young people go into the adult world with very little understanding about how finances work. They are beset on all sides with advertisements and images that tell them that they need to get the biggest, best things today - and that easy credit is available to help them to buy these things even if they can't truly afford them. With no concept of ideas like late payment fees or variable interest rates, it's very easy to find yourself in over your head with just a few purchases. These youthful mistakes can lead to a lifetime of problems for people who simply don't understand what they can do to get out of debt.

Finally, there are the more willing participants in the cycle of debt. They make purchases knowing that they'll never be able to pay for the things that they buy, but this doesn't bother them. Instead of saving for things, they mortgage off their future - it's the problem of the person who has to deal with it ten, fifteen, or even twenty years down the road. These people give in to basic consumer impulses without realizing that they are preventing themselves from generating any real wealth in the future.

Common Debt Traps

It's very easy to get into a cycle of debt, and there are certain traps that absolutely make people think that they are safe while they're really just going down in a spiral. Being able to identify these traps is not only necessary for those who want to avoid going into debt, but a smart way for people to understand how they may have fallen into debt in the first place. Looking at common debt traps is one of the best ways to understand that many people find themselves in debt not because they were foolish, but because they were misled.

Perhaps the most common trap is falling into the cycle of getting loans to pay off debts. Payday loans are particularly predatory, because they tend to make sure that borrowers get in a cycle of borrowing in order to deal with debts - you take out a single high interest loan to cover an emergency, and you'll find yourself paying far more than you expected just to cover that loan. That, in return, puts you in financial jeopardy - and you'll find yourself returning to the lender again and again just to bail yourself out.

Other common traps involve not just lending, but spending. Credit card companies are notorious for advertising to young people who have no idea how the cards really work, giving them higher spending limits than is necessary and adding in a number of fees along with a high interest rate. Once a card is maxed out, a young person who is just beginning his or her career may find himself or herself unable to make payments - thus adding on not only extra fees, but reducing his or her credit score. This will lead to higher interest rates on future loans and cards, leading to a cycle of debt that is very hard to break without the proper instruction and help.

Chapter 2: How Debt Impacts You

Sure, anyone can get into debt - it's an accepted part of life. But what's so bad about it? If you look around at the world, you'll notice that far more people are in debt than are debt-free. Indeed, going into debt seems like one of the truest signs that you're participating actively and openly within a society. While this is true, that doesn't mean that there aren't some very major downsides to going into debt - as well as some crippling realities related to being in extreme debt. Debt changes not just the way that you interact with the world, but it puts astonishing limitations on your future.

The Pitfalls of Debt

Debt is, at its heart, about much more than owing another person or entity money. Debt, at its core, is about not having complete control over your finances. The day that you go into debt, whether on purpose or by necessity, is the day when you begin to involve another party in your own financial future. In most cases, this third party has no vested interest in your happiness or your prosperity - their only goal is to make as much money off of you as possible, for as long as possible. The pitfall of debt, then, is entering into a parasitic relationship in which you willingly give control of at least a portion of your wealth to someone or something that does not have your best interest at heart.

Debt's pitfalls can be divided into three main categories - the financial, the psychological, and the potential. Each of these pitfalls plays out in a very different way, but each is just as important as the last. Understanding that your debt will have an impact on your life beyond the payments that you make today is not just a good reason to avoid going into debt, but a chance to understand that getting out of debt quickly is your best chance to take control over your life.

The Financial Impact

The most commonly cited impact of debt is the financial impact of taking out a loan. A debt is not getting money for nothing - it's simply shifting your responsibility to pay from one payee to another. While you're certainly gaining more time to pay by getting a loan, you're also entering into a much more adversarial financial relationship. Your relationship with the person to whom you need to make your initial payments is essentially equal - you need their product or service, and they need your money. The financial relationship between you and a lender, however, is not equal - you need the money much more than they need to lend it out to you.

The financial impact of going into debt generally tends to center around interest. Many people assume that lenders simply lend out money to borrowers, and somehow sustain a business by having that money paid back to them over time. That might work when you borrow money from your parents, but financial lenders make their money off of interest. They're lending you money, to be sure, but they're making a profit by charging you a premium for the amount of money that you borrow. That interest rate can eat into your wealth incredibly quickly. It's not uncommon to see payday loan rates of over twenty-five percent, for example, and it's certainly not uncommon to find that one has paid thousands of dollars more for a house when taking out a mortgage instead of paying in cash.

Financially speaking, debt tends to set up a cycle. One goes into debt, and then has less purchasing power. That lack of purchasing power, in turn, makes it far more likely that a person will continue to stay in debt. The first time that you borrow money is almost certainly not going to be your last, and it requires a strong will and a solid game plan for a person to escape debt. That's why it's not only important to understand the financial impact of debt, but to respect how much it can change your life.

The Psychological Impact

The psychological impact of debt can be astounding. Even in a perfect world, there's something horrific about having a huge financial burden on your shoulders. Those in debt tend to be more likely to be depressed, irritable, and anxious. Money troubles split up marriages and turn families against one another, all while doing little to alleviate the problems actually caused by debts.

The world, of course, is not perfect. Many people in debt fall behind, and this puts them in the sights of debt collectors. You might already be aware of the late night and early morning phone calls, the threatening letters, and the potential law suits that are just around the corner. This helps to promote an atmosphere for anxiety and dread, leaving those in debt more worried and more frightened than their debt-free peers.

The Potential Impact

Debt also hobbles your potential in life. Interest payments reduce not just your current buying power, but reduce your buying power in the future. Money you pay towards your debt is money that doesn't go into your retirement account, that doesn't pay for those family vacations, and that doesn't help you to move into a new home. Money tied up in debt makes it harder for you to invest, harder for you to buy, and even harder for you to borrow in the future.

The real secret - and the biggest pitfall - of debt is that it follows you and prevents your future from being as bright as it could be. You might spend hundreds or thousands of dollars a month on interest-only payments, only to find that you make no headway. This will stop you from saving in the future, and stop you from living the kind of life that you deserve to have. Debt is a shackle that will weigh you down when you deserve to soar towards a better, brighter future.

Chapter 3: Solving Your Debt Problem Without Borrowing

Paying off debts requires nothing more than cold, hard, cash. This is great for those people who have a rich uncle or a trust fund to fall back on - you can just borrow from someone else to take care of your problems. There are two major issues with this. First, you're simply transferring your debt from one place to another - from a creditor to a relative, in some cases, or from your present to your future. The other major issue is that it fails to solve the root problem of how you got into debt - you're still borrowing money that you have to pay back. Your goal shouldn't just be to eliminate your debt - it should be to take care of the problem on your own so that you don't have to live through the nightmare that is dealing with excessive debt in the future. You need to create a mechanism for making more money - and you need to do it in such a way that you can pay off your debts without generating any more.

Strategies for Reducing Debt

If you've made it this deep into the book, you'll notice that a lot of the world of debt happens to revolve around making plans - or the failure to do so. That's not a coincidence - planning is going to be a huge part of what you are going to do from now on. You didn't plan to get into a massive amount of debt, but you're certainly going to plan to get out of debt. This takes more than just a few good thoughts and a determined attitude - you're going to get to work on your new strategies as quickly as possible.

As you might imagine, one doesn't just jump into the world of reducing debt without a game plan. There are several really great ways to plan on getting rid of your debt, but you've got to start out by figuring out how you're going to raise a little bit of extra money. The three options below are three of the best ways to raise cash for your attempts to get rid of your debts.

Option One: Part-time jobs

It shouldn't be surprising that one of the best ways to deal with your debt is to make more money. Unfortunately, getting a raise at your current job is likely out of your hands - and in an economy that doesn't always value hard work, it's unlikely that you'll be able to convince your boss to shell out a little extra in order to help you with your problems. Fortunately, you do have another option - you can get a part time job to help you pay off your debt. You don't have to keep it forever, but you can use it to give yourself a financial boost when you are in a tough situation.

Getting a second job is a good deal easier when you've got a steady schedule, but almost anyone can find a way to make a little bit of extra money if they are willing to give up a bit of their time. If you work the typical forty hour week, you've got at least two days a week off - and that means you've got extra time to make a little extra cash. Your second job doesn't have to be as labor-intensive or as time-consuming as your main job, but the goal of holding this kind of employment should be to divert all of your new funds into the elimination of your debt. Even if you only make an extra hundred dollars a week, you are looking at fifty-two hundred dollars that you can put towards your debt each year.

Part-time jobs with a degree of self-direction are ideal for this strategy. Something like delivering pizza usually requires you to work hours that are outside of the typical nine-to-five grind, but can allow you to make a fair deal of money during your usual leisure time. While there's certainly nothing particularly fun about having to take on a second job in order to deal with your debt, it can allow you to focus on slowly wearing down that mountain of money that you owe to other people.

Option Two: Starting a side business

Of course, not everyone needs to go out and find a job that will pay them pennies. Some people have natural - or learned - talents that they can use to pick up money on the side. People will pay for almost any task, and those that start a side business can rake in quite a bit of extra money by doing something that they enjoy - or at least, for which they have the tools. Side businesses can range from mowing lawns to working as a ghost writer, but they are a great way to provide you with a little extra motivation while you work on eliminating your debt.

Side businesses take a good deal more effort to get moving than a typical part-time job, but they have the potential to make you much more money. Since you're working for yourself, every penny that the business earns can be put back into getting rid of your debt. You don't have to worry about waiting for pay day or hoping that you get the right hours - you set your schedule, and you can deal with the profits on your own terms. You might even find that your side business is profitable enough to become your primary job -

that is, after you are done paying down your debt. Like the part-time job, a side business is meant to exist as a second revenue stream instead of as a method of replacing your primary way of making money.

The one warning about starting a side business is this: it absolutely must have a low overhead, or you are going to find yourself in even more financial trouble in the future. While it's certainly likely that you will have to make at least one or two major purchases to get your business off the ground, you don't need to go into more debt to start making money. That's why certain businesses - computer repair, lawn care, etc. - tend to make use of equipment that the owner already has around the house. Your goal is to eliminate your debt, not to create more problems for yourself by spending money.

Option Three: Selling items that you own but no longer need

In debt or not, there's a good chance that you own more things than you need. People are creatures of habit and tend to like to keep old things around - even if they're not useful. As the saying goes, one man's trash is another man's treasure. If you can take the time to go through everything that you own, you should find that you have more than a few items that are worth money to other people. If you can force yourself to part with these items, you can add a bit to your store of cash and turn that money towards paying down part of your debt.

If you're honest, you know that this step is probably one that has been a long time coming. Think back to all the yard sales and rummage sales that you've been to - or even held

- in the past. These simple sales are one of the most uniquely American ways to get rid of the clutter in your home, allowing you to turn a tidy profit by giving your neighbors a chance to poke through all of your stuff. The only difference between your attempts to get rid of your clutter and those of your neighbors is that you're going to try to turn that money towards getting rid of the debt that has accumulated over the years.

Don't be afraid to go online for this step, because you might actually be able to make a fair bit of money by doing so. A quick look at some online auction or classifieds websites will show you that your junk really is treasure to some people - and you can command a higher price when people are looking for a specific item. Be sure to pay careful attention to when these websites are offering specials for sellers, especially when they will let you sell an item for no cost. If you're willing to navigate the world of online auction sites, you should be able to find a way to turn some of your old items into more fuel for your debt-reducing fire.

What's important to remember about all three of these strategies is this - you aren't making extra money, you are eliminating debt. It can feel great to have a bit of extra cash, especially if you are already in the process of putting every spare dime into your existing debts. What you have to do, though, is to fight the urge to consider this money to be yours for the spending - it's just a quicker, more expedient way to pay down the amount you owe. If you can break the cycle of spending what you don't have, you can break the cycle of debt.

Chapter 4 – Debt Elimination Strategies

Once you've got your extra money rolling in, you've got to take a good, hard look at your situation. Debt elimination strategies are universal, but every debt is different. Some debts can be discharged through bankruptcy, while others will stick with you through thick and thin. Some debts need to be paid quickly, while others will allow you to do so over time. No matter what, the debt will hang around your neck like the proverbial albatross - and you'll have to do whatever you can to make sure that you can remove it quickly and efficiently.

It's easy to think of the three steps below as different strategies, as each can be used successfully on its own to help to eliminate all of your debt. If you really want to get through the process and out on the other side, you'll need to make use of all three strategies. Don't be fooled by the relative ease of the first step either - going through the process of debt elimination is one that's going to hit you right in your lifestyle, and it's going to hurt. However, the rewards are more than worth the effort that you put in.

Step One: Debt snowball strategy

Think for a moment of how you make a snowman. Those giant snowballs don't come fully formed - they take a good deal of hard work, and a very specific method of creation. You start with a tiny snowball, perhaps no bigger than your hand. Bit by bit, you add to it - more snow, more ice, and more effort. In time, that tiny snowball becomes the base of something that's much bigger. In time, it becomes a foundation on which you can build something impressive. That's the basic philosophy behind making the debt snowball.

A debt snowball starts simply - you look at the people to whom you owe money, and figure out what the smallest debt on which you are paying might be. This is easier for those people who are already making monthly payments on their debts, because they've made some headway towards paying off at least part of some the money that they owe. Once you've identified the smallest of your debts, you put all the extra money that you've made above towards paying off that smaller amount. Depending on the debt, you can get this done in a relatively short amount of time. There's no time to celebrate though, because you're going to need to move on.

Once you've paid off your smallest debt, you move on to the next debt. The only difference is that you're now adding the amount of money that you were paying each month to the smallest debt to the next in line. If you were paying twenty-five dollars a month towards one debt and you've paid it off, you can turn around and start putting that same twenty-five dollars a month towards the next debt - along with the money that you make from your part-time job or your side business. This allows you to slowly but surely dedicate more money to each debt payment, all while maintaining the same kind of budget that you were using before.

Step Two: Budgeting and extreme saving

Your debt snowball should be a huge part of your debt repayment process, and there's no doubt about that. Outside of the snowball, though, you've got to start finding ways to add more money to those monthly payments. When you are in debt, it's not the amount that you owe that tends to really hurt you - it's the interest. For some, paying off debts just a month or two faster can not only help them to get out from under the specter of debt collectors, but can also save them thousands of dollars. If you want to make sure that you are actually saving money, there's only one way to get through the process - you've got to find ways to make more out of what you already have.

The first thing you need to do, of course, is to create a budget. You have to figure out exactly how much money you need to spend in a given month - and, of course, how much you can start saving. There are certain things that you're going to have to pay, of course - you've got to pay your rent or mortgage, as well as your utility bills. Those things are non-negotiable, but you'll find that much of what you spend your money on is incredibly unnecessary. Once you get the budget down, you'll have to do one of the hardest things in the world - you'll have to actually take the time to sit down and live with it.

If you really want to save money by eliminating your debts quickly, you'll have to jump into the always frightening world of extreme saving. The vast majority of what you spend money on is not a necessity, no matter how much you might think that it is. Get ready to cut out your cable bill, switch over to slower internet speeds and switch your smartphone and its unlimited data plan out for a pre-paid phone with no internet service. You're going to make life harder on yourself, but you're going to put all of that extra money where it's going to be better used - into paying off your debts. You get your luxuries back when you can afford them.

Step Three: Downsizing

If you didn't think that going all-out to make sure that you could save money was hard enough, now you're in for the real kicker of saving money - it's time for you to start downsizing your life. You cut out all the luxuries, and that's tough - but the third step is making things really, really hard. You're going to look at everything around you, and figure out how you can reduce it to the bare minimum of livability. Yes, that means you're going to get ready for some hard times today so that you can have some great times tomorrow.

You need to turn a critical eye towards your life for this step, trying to figure out what you can reduce in order to have more money to put towards your debts. For some, that means getting rid of things, as above - but instead of meaningless items around your house, it means getting rid of things that might actually matter. That means going from two cars to one, or selling that lovely boat that you love so much. You're going to be looking for a way simplify your life in such a manner that you not only generate more cash, but that you eliminate as much of the outgoing money as possible from your life.

In short, you're going to downsize. Have the kids moved out, but you still have a big house? Sell it, buy a cheaper home and throw that extra money that you've made towards your debts. Are you spending hundreds of dollars a month at the grocery store? Get ready to go down to rice and beans for a while, and put the extra cash towards your credit card bills. Is this extreme? Absolutely. It's also one of the best ways to get rid of all the extra expenditures in your life so that you can finally get rid of your debts.

It's incredibly hard to make these recommendations to the average person, because it doesn't always feel like it is worthwhile. If you're comfortable - not happy, but comfortable - with your debts, it can be hard to feel like you are punishing yourself just to eliminate a few numbers on a page. In reality though, these steps are a good way to make sure that you are going to be able to really live the life that you want to live in the future. If you have to, buy a whiteboard and write down exactly how much debt you have - and when you're feeling down about your changes, make sure to update that whiteboard to show how much money you've managed to pay off by just living a bit more cheaply. If you're really willing to put in all the hard work and to undertake a little bit of suffering in order to get back on the right track, you'll be able to experience all of the benefits that come with living debt free.

Chapter 5 – Benefits of working hard to become debt free

If you've read through the steps you need to take to eliminate debt and the strategies you must employ, you've got to be wondering why you should even bother. Those are some pretty extreme steps - and they'll make your life very miserable in the short term. Fortunately, working hard to become debt free really does change the way that you live your life. Understanding the benefits will help you to become a long-term planner, and should help you to put even more energy into avoiding debt in the future. All it takes is a little optimism and a look at the lives of those who live without debt.

Let's start out with the obvious - getting out of debt just feels good. Imagine life without those phone calls, without the letters, and without the idea of someone breathing down your neck. Imagine life knowing that everything that you have is something that you really own, that no bank or lender can take away. How great would it be to know that you don't owe a penny to anyone else, that you get to keep everything that you make? How relaxing would it be to know that when your paycheck comes in, that it all goes back to your family? That's what living debt free can do for you.

You should also note that being debt free drastically increases your buying power. Think of how much of your budget today goes towards making those debt payments. Once you're done paying your debts, you make the same amount of money - but now, it doesn't have to go to someone else. You've got the ability to really save for the first time in your life, to put aside money for your future and to watch it grow. You get to reap the fruits of your own labor for once, instead of sending most of it off to a bank or to a lender.

There's also the fact that you can finally afford those luxuries that you had to deny yourself. When you're in debt, luxuries are something to be avoided - you can't afford them, because your money needs to go elsewhere. Once you're out of debt, you can start spending wisely. You can have the cable hooked back up, and get a reasonable car - all without having to borrow a dime. You have the chance to live a fantastic life that those who are in debt simply cannot imagine.

You also have the chance to have a real, meaningful impact with your money. No debt means setting up and funding college savings accounts for your children. It means putting away enough money to travel when you retire. It also means having the money to help other people - not just to loan someone a dollar or two, but to help out with the causes that you have always wanted to support. If you don't have to worry about your debts, you can start putting your money to work in the most wonderful ways.

Chapter 6 – Strategies for staying debt free

Once you have your debts behind you, your journey isn't over. In many ways, you're setting yourself up on a new financial adventure - one that should not involve debt. You have to learn not just to spend your money wisely, but to watch out for the possibility of debt in the future. Once you don't have those debts on your back, though, you will find the process much easier. Instead of worrying about how you will pay your bills, you'll be on the lookout for how to secure your future in ways that makes sense for you. Below are three great rules that you can follow.

Rule #1: Always Pay in Cash

Once you're debt free, you'll find yourself in a unique position. You will not have a mortgage or a car payment. You'll still pay utilities and have living expenses, but you won't have to deal with those payments that really take a lot of money out of your paycheck. That means that you can save - and that you don't need to borrow. From this point forward, make sure that you never pay for anything on credit. If you can't afford it, just wait - your savings will grow. As a rule, you should never buy anything that you cannot afford today.

Rule #2: Keep an Emergency Fund

Related to Rule #1, one of your biggest goals should be to keep an emergency fund that will last you for at least ninety days. That means you need to have enough money in your savings to not only pay for your utilities bills, but your reasonable living expenses, for three months. This will allow you to weather any kind of financial emergency without having to run to a lender, and will help you to deal with unexpected expenses by drawing on your own money instead of having to go to a lender.

Rule #3: Always Pay Yourself

Finally, you'll need to remember that your first goal is to pay yourself. You might be tempted to buy something that you can only barely afford, but remember that you and your family come before anything that you can buy. This means paying your utility bills and food bills first - anything that is left should be first saved, and then spent if there is anything left. If you get into the habit of always paying yourself first, it will become easier to avoid impulse purchases.

Conclusion

Living life without debt is simply a matter of making smart monetary decisions and keeping your guard up. If you remember all the hard work you had to do to dig yourself out from that mountain of debt, you'll be surprised how easy it is to avoid going back to that kind of life. With time, you'll begin to see debt for what it really is - not something that makes your life easier, but rather an obstacle in the way of your future happiness and your prosperity. You have all the tools you need to fight debt - you just have to choose to use them.

www.ingramcontent.com/pod-product-compliance
Lightning Source LLC
Chambersburg PA
CBHW020716180526
45163CB00008B/3110